I'm Your Field Trip

poems

by Katharine Polenberg

2008 PolekatBooks
Copyright© 2008 by Katharine Polenberg

ISBN: 978-0-6151-8807-2

All rights reserved under International and Pan American Copyright Conventions. Published in the United States by PolekatBooks and lulu Press.

original cover art: Katharine Polenberg

Grateful acknowledgements are due to the editors of the following publications where some of these poems first appeared:

Laura Hird
Cerebral Catalyst
thieves jargon
Zygote In My Coffee
Poor Mojos Almanac(k)
Cherry Bleeds
Outsider Writers
Idiom Magazine

Library of
Congress Cataloging-in-Publication Data

Dedication:

For my Howie
my Jessie & Becky

my brothers

and my friends

CONTENTS:

some fifty-odd pages of poems I wrote and a cover illustration I painted (Duh, haven't you been paying attention?)

I'm Your Field Trip

I am millions of dollars of
technology and science
you forget
when you look
that you're seeing this
new appliance
I am THAT good

When I move
steel bone under
poly resin flesh
it's seamless
I'm smooth as
thunder is
powdered sugar
no less like
this morning waving
at cars
only half-dressed

Hissing compressed air
with every breath I take
when you're awake
Ingersoll Rand
had a hand
in delivering the motion
I can't really be

fathomed more-
like a non-Newtonian shearing force
or how big is the ocean?

how do they know
what sound I
would have made?

they dug up the skulls
of ancestors
and turned on
a tape recorder
and blew into the
sockets bone

What you're hearing
is just vibration caused
when your hot breath
meets my still force of
elemental stone

Take what you hear
leave the rest alone

That Day I Quit the Circus

I heard the screaming
first I was there
taking the matter
into my own hands
when it did land
I slapped it
alive
I admit it

dove in where the
action always is
the Big Top
center ring

the hanging trapeze
midwives pissed off
on strike cause
their act is cut
with scissors
into little
dainty doilies
don't stare
but if you
look hard
they fold like poodles
and midgets

the air
inside the tent got

hot and danger
filled with flying
pinking shears
snipping pretty
the kamikaze clowns
cut the cord
opening a whole other
context for
their act
to fall through

after that it got ugly
it got real messy
when they folded up
the tent and took it
on the road
looking for a
booking the
scissors juggler
circus midwives with poodle
hair bitching sisters

this is
no place for a man
mister you best
make for the door
I fainted myself
dead on the floor
cause no fucking way
was I mopping
this one up

Was a "Method" Actor

Raised by wolves on Marlon Brando movies
do you remember how you made
a cool million sounding like every fireworks finale
and Titanic distress flares like ripping open
a Velcro tennis elbow
pad ticktickticktickrrrrip from down here
in the radio room of the rescue boat
and every undocumented dark face was
assumed trustworthy so you
didn't need a kickstand
to lean plans on
and rest and rock and roll smoked like a
punk before someone weeded out the cat
tails and run-on sentences of gothic proportions and epic
importance torn from
composition notebooks fit
through the little vent slots in locker doors
that was before the
sending districts consolidated how you wore
your street clothes in updated stealthy swatches after
class when you felt free to chase me
when I ran on like that God—

Slower Approach to Yellow

I can't stand
any place
except right here
not touching (mind you)
but near
enough
to the old stuffed ones
now they have wound themselves up

into one big
balled clog
in your carotid coffee
your slip-knotted noose
your loose vertical razor cuts
across intersecting
sippycup streets and
microbrew avenues
and mid-sentence . . .

. . . trails off

because their "real kids"
(the ones I dream I'm doing away with)

keep crossing
in between
against my light

makes me want to red scream

Please Don't Tap on the Glass

finally I went
selectively mute
only sound effects erupt
pop my frame
pointy
crime-scene yellow
flash of injury
hurts
my eyes
empty balloons hover
friend-of-a-friend awkward
and you
look chicken wire cut up
partitioned in squares
from my side
of the window
I can read your thought
cloud whisper

"This is no fucking joke, is it Doc?"

with all my ink I try to tell you:

"I'm a comic strip"

while you sit

passive and tapping

selectively

reading me

What's His Problem?

He always finishes me off like a church service
like the pause before we announce the winner
of this years award for outstanding
after this next clip
breathes in his own heroic breath to pronounce me:

"I got all the decay, but you have to be diligent from now
on because. . .
There Is No More Forever!"

Now why'd he have to say that?
In this fancy fourth floor sweet god knows how many chairs
with a hygienist who makes me watch fucking
Anna Nicole Smiths C section on E! ("she's so pretty and
soooo messed up")
while he drills away my last expectation of immortality
from my insensate mouth while I'm wishing they'd let me
spy out the window on the FineFare parking lot Nazi
across the street rubbing his 5 x 8 crack'n peal
red warning sticker onto my Buicks windshield cuz he
knows

I didn't take the cart into the store and he knows
I know he saw me ditch it behind the medical arts building
and I wish HE was my dentist

Because he has infinity

of these red warning stickers:
Parking Is For Customers Only

and he would never dream of telling me
"forever" isn't true
and I'll lose that tooth still owing five hundred dollars

but at least I'll die before I pay that Nazi off

I Like To Drown

currently I'm sticky-shiny
with dirt sweet and sweaty hi-gloss hurt
licked my cuts I taste me
I need salt, I should bathe
I should swim, take a dip

it was a trip, I hitched to the ocean
her open-wound tractor-groomed
beachfront and gave myself to water
that waves and won't let me walk away

got tired and cold
got up and out against a rip-tide
facing away from the moon's shimmering pride
well-hung globe
but she won't let me walk away

she had my calf gripped in a wave fist
lapping she grabbed at my ankles
I pulled out and she licked my heels

I wear them high now
as tidal waves
and step high and brave
but she won't let me walk away

I just spilled the milk here
the whole gallon of pasteurized ocean
linoleum beached (and yes I cried over it)
briefly—

the hi-gloss wet white laps at my heels
though, I tasted my ankle and I need salt
sticky-shiny I should bathe (or swim) she
won't let me walk away

Lake Of Cows

she tells her story
a lake of spilled water:
not enough history to wash
the fake name
of man-made vacations
swimming in white
dreams sleeping fornication
a rampant mid-century rape
on clean mud dirtied
a good lake still
she wasn't born there

planted she sprung
from earth given in to cave
in on its indigenous face
her veins dug open and tapped
well with dollars folded to
shovel shape
to intrude and scoop

and gut out her worm stories
and stone energy and anthill industry
by their roots and make
a septic hole of still water

fed on cow dung
and steeped in the parched
blood of creatures bleached
bones splitting and spilling
a graphite marrow

she had long worn a
wild towhead of witch hazel
yellow plaited until
tractors combed and parted her smooth
making first pasture into hothouse soil
for propagating market-ready meat
roiling on packed and weighed
down foundations poured

once strong now gasping
a mineral breath
exorcised stones muscles flexed
virile land worked for
developed resorts honeymoon nest
on the new roads

under heeled and spurred
diamond-cut legs and calf
in less than half the old walking
distance for the white
hand fisted around wads
of fresh-minted "green frog skins"
they call money
in the bank free flowing
rolling in like unknotted hemp lasso

how their unkempt mother grew
split-level homes she
cradled to sleep on a lakefront dream
while she cried volcanic
tears over the flood
they named the new water
in her native tongue
and it was a lie

but the people did buy there
and brought forth their next children
on false belief and genuine thirst
for more room the
real estate had boomed loud

and crowds of kid
feet rooted loosely
in new laid sod would roam
paw and aimlessly drink
with brothers in the wood that still stood
while the conception of immaculate
water this lake holds her own
council still waters

the only life
that a sister has left to tell siblings
these old stories of their own
cradles to their graves

One Hit Wonder

how does that one go?
it starts with the final note
DEcomposition is everything

it's a gift
giving up
to the elements
all at once let's sing the whole show
one song one note too low
equalized on a cellular level
sounds like this:

airport pilot-ready
high alert
only library carpet square
and lawn chair
steady
flag down mailbox broken
jaw open
three-legged dog
shadow Lincoln Log
wood treated in
red-handed boy
history
hemp-color molded plastic
unbreakable

seamlessly
crop circle dead grass under
backyard
trampoline

high tight elastic pony tail whips
sweat flattened yellow bangs drip -

drive-by crawl line news
push-button ice cubes
water pressure froth
drain clog bath

what I'm saying . . . is "LAUGH!"

it's the whole show
one song one note
decomposition riff
is a gift

A Good Cook

hows that old lady get up & down

her creaky steep steps?

it ain't easy-

if she slept

she freaks herself

out of twilight cherry

Sucrets trinket box wakes blinking

a code to the dog who gets it the state

she's in she writes auto-bio notes to expired

milkmen in case- just in case- she looks up the

recipe again on corn-yellow coupon for do-it-your

self spitshine his pickled dong ding! time she's a keeper

of a rubber

band drawer household

and poor recall for all that

she will after all still soak her

red cabbage in Happy Valentines Day!

Jean Nate' stock and flabbergast a tuna

she filleted with a crochet hook putting in

eyelet lace for good taste hiding her Philips head

screw-driven mind in her apron bib she's cooking in

fearless aroma

keeps it turning how

she learned bag-heavy

purple steps she walks up

by heart in the dark treads she

keeps broom clean sweep of everything

but turned up odd button beads she might need

saves those up too with her half-baked

aroma of sooner or later

he comes out of his

weekly coma

and eats her

sunday supper

Outsider Artist

they say we corrupt

everything we touch

then

we will only touch what is

already corrupt

we'll spit on our shirt tails and

scrub up a sliver

of our reflection

naked we'll plane with calloused skin

a knot hole smooth

ashes we'll drift and settle

a mote upon some earth

and for some time

we'll fertilize . . .

Yeah but, what if

If I agree to paint you naked
wearing a rented pirate costume
and picture you walking (like a dog) on a short leash
a choke-chained tube of raw cookie dough
and if I agree to PhotoShop away the
tomato paste scabs

on your shirt and also blur
every place where flagellation scars show
and if I agree to pee on a bonfire or into a
compost pit while at the same time

I rip out my tongue (or yours if you prefer) and
single-handedly fan it dry like it's a vacation-trip Polaroid
snapshot at the same time I'm still making eye contact

or if I give you only two (not three) of these scenarios that
rhyme for example then
then will you

agree to frame me
and mount me
and hang me
in your foyer and call me artist

and *finally* admit
you're poetry?

Color of Waiting

bird nest dead

house paint on iron

rusting red

copper leaf shutters

whistle mountain train

through random scattered

buckshot mouths

peripheral distance coming close

pour lava in my thermos

light a brush fire rolled

between my lips

a season is

waiting.

Rather have a bottle in front of me . . .

lather
rinse
repeat
just like that
keep it neat mental
hygiene projected onto a
green screen lather rinse repeat
it's ECT lather it's shampoo treatment
it's conditioner rinse it's not what you think

rinse
it's not lather
it's white and sticky
dry like some near-sighted
dick-lexic oral rapist with bad aim

.

repeat
shot his jizz
all in your hair at
the temples while you were asleep
lather
gather yourself
together it's only Vaseline

from where the electrodes were applied
rinse
that delivered
the therapeutic 30 second
seizure rather simple really it's to cure you

repeat
of this kind of
delusion that you've been
having you're brain lathered, rinsed, repeat raped

lather

rinse

repeat

Power Surge

Above the blue flame
in the smallest pot
the surface skin
begins
to pucker quietly-

"Put your socks and shoes
and any jewelry
in the paper bag"

I remind myself
not to sit here
with my foot up
my ankle crossed over
my knee
I don't want them to see
not yet so it's a shock
for the doc when I get in there . . .

-Soft white puckers turn
to blisters
that bubble and bounce
popping like whispers
passing through a
well-behaved
audience or
waiting room
of patients

in pharmaceutical restraint
not the violent
six point restraint
head, waist, feet, hands
sleepy whispers
raining spittle
on the stovetop
better stir-

"Hop up here and lay down
you're next"
Ah . . . finally
the needle
the best part
about treatment for "psychotic depression"
is the vicarious death
by lethal injection
delivered weekly
the friendly anesthetist
makes light comfort noises
as she takes me through

the countdown

from one hundred . . . ninety-nine . . . ninety-eight . . .
nine-seve- and (I'm out and my toes do the curl-dance
that signals the voltage applied to my brain inside
through to my temporal lobes passed skin and skull
has caused the thirty seconds
seizure

has virtually overturned and shaken the crude traces
of my own face clean off my etch-a-sketch memory
made me a clean slate . . .

-A wooden spoon dives
into the pot
skimming the sticky stuff
from the insides
a hand attached to my self
but not my will

spirals the spoon
to the center
bulls eye
the biggest bubbles
now a boil
white splotches scab up
into sepia brown
on the enamel around

the burner-

The headache after ECT
can't be easily fathomed or soothed
or defended against beforehand
(like with a hangover preventive)
it is truly splitting
no one really knows what that means
unless they are coming back
into their scalp to look out
their eyes again after the third or
thirtieth shock treatment . . .

-Not all back
in my body yet
just my head
and a careful
inching crawl
down into my hair
I'm a slack-jawed clown
with no motor control
I knock the wooden spoon
from the pot

At my feet and I can
laugh at this
my toes
still baring the faces
of the ten little

curl-dancers
with their snotty slogans
I inked on too
the balls of my feet
epithets to the doctor
and his toe-watching helpers
nothing I can repeat
in polite company

My feet!
wave to me
I smile back
because
I JUST NOW DECIDED
to waive the warm milk
of my quiet future

and run
loudly outside
with my
impatient bare feet
grabbing at
the distance
electrified with freedom!

A Closet Concert

you are invited to sit down
with me and eat
on the corner
where the quarter round
and sheet rock meet

where the plank boys
make their loud singing noise
as their open mouths roar
I see them ingrained
in the pine wood floor

I hear music in milled
lumber where it stops still
at the door sill calling
ants to come over through
the daylight crack as sirens wail

they set up tiny drums
brought in on their backs
on the flat head nails
that are

wrongly driven
to keep me mute

and hidden

and in my place

Introduction to Music

the first music I ever watched
before I could hear
before I could read

was music made by typesetters
back when it was hot type
their hands knew more than their eyes
where the letters are in the typecase
plucking and picking the punctuation
composing the words into sentences and
making paragraph spaces and mastheads
hot wax sounded jazzy
the pressman loading rolls of
newsprint , I mean rolls without end
always more written and letters cast
paper cutters razor percussions swoop
ink sounding loud in black and
singing along to color on the comic page
rubber cement and nonrepro blue pencil on

invisible graph come in and the pressroom is exploding now
with glory
of music

to a person kneehigh to
a roll of newsprint

just tall enough to drop a dime
in the vending machine for a root beer
and that sweet candy taste
and the sound of money drop
stops the music in a kids head
who finds hey I've been sweating I needed that!

Just what I hear when the sunday paper
hits the porch door and coffees ready to pour.

Damn Lucky

If I am lucky
my yellow kitchen tiles
(the ones my friends hate because
they're dangerously cracked)
plan out their salt licked blue music
over night while I sleep
to flat people voices
and stealth carpet noises

If I'm lucky
they start in singing
right when the coffee pot
breathes steam into the grout
and makes the drywall sneeze and giggle
and blow its nose on a coffee filter
before it lets the yellow singing come out

Then if I'm lucky
my cup heats up to a band sound
so loud it tastes like the neighbors
are watching the weather report
on a big TV that smells like

tapping aspirin out of a bottle
for some arthritis in the knee while
my kitchen harmony over here goes running
out to their curtain rods
drumming up a throaty red
dog leash unwinding in the yard

And when I'm lucky the humming
coming from my silverware drawer
strikes a note on the belt
buckle and the mailbox hinge
of the people next door so that

If we are lucky
we bump into each other while
whistling along to the same one track
this morning catching a train
we are sharing a breakfast of
a musically disordered brain
that causes singing in common things
like what happened today

Exactly that way, so what can I say
except that I am damn lucky!

Asbury Park Tattoo

Dear, ain't life grand
on the promenade?
kids, hold my hand
and we'll wink and nod

at them two writing their wills
by writing their names
on his hairy flesh
between the arcade games

this tattoo parlor
makes the wedding vow
of illegal unions
right here and now
with red and blue ink buzzing in
to his underage skin

"For eighty bucks
get two names
in script with a heart!"
they walked down
the boardwalk aisle
swearing they'll never part

she's down on the alter
of 90 degree heat
wearing a pink halter top
and flip flops on her feet

they honeymoon tonight
and then pack it in
because in two weeks, Man!
the new school year begins

now we all know love
recedes with the tide
and all they know is they got
school supplies to buy

their vows stay dark
and hidden under his jeans
right up until her prom dress
bursts at the seams

what? Come on!
they're young and
it was hot
and anyway, folks
what else have they got?

Story of my pants:

caught my pants talking this morning
one leg said to the other

jean what's wrong. . . you look like you got cuffed or some such

jean said -

just blue is all. . .feel stiff. . . don't like our knee-hole like I used to. . .do you still love our asshole the same . . .are we at that age?

other leg folded cause he did know what to say

that age when you wake up not dead and figure it's too late now to die young and too soon
too hard
too time-consuming to snap

pair of pants talked for a longer time after that. . . mostly about how they don't like having to work the zipper fly and wanting to not die

that's when I couldn't listen anymore and put them on to go to the store

. . . the TRUTH?

I hate fucking fake indians
and immodest women
yes- the damage is already done
I hate them

reminding me
in shapes of theft and apology
words

from fish scale glitter lips
plucked whiskers land
in my shower where they stick up
and stab bare unsuspecting feet
like mine

their tiny
curly black spines
you find in cottage cheese
might bite

my tongue too
if I didn't see this coming
in the piles of dirty underwear

I hate immodest lying

fake indians
and women
who laugh out loud and hug
their infantalized boyfriends
suck
the life out of witnesses

with dead batteries
that means the remote has to go without
I have to get up
to change the channel or else

fall
asleep with hate and
lip gloss makeover shows and
missing Phil Donahue
who I hate too
because she comes on my screen
every day

Paris Hilton promising me
nothing will ever matter

Pork Roll Justice

maybe this was some
hoo doo
or maybe just some jersey style
Fuck You but
here's what she did:

when the sheriff took her
from her house
she hid

a whole raw pork roll
with a pig face
she hand-carved in

she stuck it up with a shiv
in the ceiling behind her pantry
so it would rot
behind the wall

while their contractors and
decorators gutted it all

her history flesh bone
and plastered
her home cooked smell
in a Dumpster

but they were leaving
her pantry intact they said
like Martha Stewart it has charm

they had no idea
cuz now there's some alarm

in their voices at night
"What IS that stench?" they moan

it's just grandma saying

"Fuck you

and welcome home!"

Heyoka

If you wake up okay tomorrow
(and I'm not saying that I think you won't)

and you said that you really "want it"
when you really meant that you don't

and sticks make pinatas horny
and concrete tans the earths' bare hide
and turtles hunt coyotes for sporting

Well, won't you be in for a helluva ride ?

Sucks about Zombies

we have something in common
I told him
at least one thing so far:

we both hate, right?

and they say you hate what you fear, right? so okay
let's go from there

and he said I hate zombies
and I said I do too
and he also told me he is afraid of them
and so am I but why?

in my case it's for how ENORMOUSLY
and thoroughly
they've been destroyed and survived thier lives
are deformed beyond recognition
except for their clothes
which tell you who they were
and give you a clue as to what kind of hunger
they would feel like
if its a librarian zombie
or a fireman zombie in their former life

or a butcher zombie will obviously carry around a
knife and a cop zombie will probably have a gun
and be hungry for the donut shop guy and so on . . .

so zombies are predictable yet scary! and it must be
because they don't suffer well

like a ghost of a war hero with his implied glory
does or suffer colorfully with assumed untold stories
like a famous junkie who drained himself
of his own fluids because he probably
set it all to music but
regular people zombies scare us
and he compared that to . . .

. . . a lot of philosophical crap anyway
so I was getting bored and asked him

what's the scariest part about being a zombie

because he was one (I am too BTW)

and he said it's not ever knowing
what to say
and how to relate to the notundead
even with your clothes and stuff
it's like props that were from a different play
you don't know your lines
so you go around
confused and groaning and scared

so we agreed it SUCKS!

being a zombie like us for that reason
so we have two things in common now

that we hate
that we relate

to each others fears

Break Me Even

dog and cat break me even
cat came stray
okay I feed him
okay I like to love him
Fuck! he has seizures
Vet says epileptic
put cat on pheno
No fair! not even

drug store charge me five
instead of fifty bucks
their mistake he's covered
(he's not my "boy" named Chuck)
okay I'll keep him
cheap enough

now today dog looks
about ready to die
can't walk she tries and
can't stand no more
she's willing to go right
there on the floor I can't
just can't watch this
Vet says bring her

she got a needle plunger
full of lethal last frisbee
her teeth snapped fast on
that "good catch" I told her
she retrieved it home
away from me even

before her legs stop
running I tell my kids
I'm not funnin' with you
do me this way -

when my day comes I can't
stand up and run
wrap me up in a blanket
pack me in the back seat
and take me out
like my dog
for the lethal needle frisbee

put the ash in a
coffee can I don't care
but don't you dare leave
the blanket behind there
bring it back home
so I can rest knowing
I died broke even

Three Days Road

before I will walk
the three days road
just once for all time
I would like to know

sound of a fingertips' giggle
to tingle other skin
feel of loud bloodrush chant
the flush from outside in

see a dawn light through my
own muscle and bone
and leave night as one
before I start dying alone

just once for all time
I would love
to know
before I walk the three days road

Souvenir Stand –

please have your money ready

I

Thank You for Your Visit!

You are responsible for carrying out your own trash.

www.ingramcontent.com/pod-product-compliance
Lightning Source LLC
Chambersburg PA
CBHW021027090426
42738CB00007B/925